SMALL BUSINESS LOAN REQUEST GUIDE

SMALL BUSINESS LOAN REQUEST GUIDE

**Put together a presentation that gets the funds
you need for your business.**

TED NICHOLS

This book was printed in the United States of America.

Rev. date: 02\28\2013

To order additional copies of this book, contact:
Xlibris Corporation
1-888-795-4274
www.Xlibris.com
Orders@Xlibris.com
128880

CONTENTS

Introduction

This guide will help the small-business owner prepare for one of the most important efforts in the operation of their business—the application for a loan from an outside funding source such as a local bank. At some point in the early stage of the business, it becomes apparent that the initial cash invested in the business is not sufficient to cover planned business expenditures. Most new businesses are undercapitalized. The initial investment of capital will not be enough to sustain the planned operations of the business. The initial capital investment has come from a limited source of funds. Most small businesses are funded at the beginning by savings, credit cards, borrowings on home equity loans, and loans from loyal family members. A major disappointment occurs for the business owner when he or she realizes that the business concept can be successful, but a shortage of funds prevents the business from continuing with its business plan.

The next step can be both difficult and intimidating. Most banks want to see a successful business "track record" showing up to three years of profitable operations. Businesses that are less than three years old, or have not yet reached the bank's standards for profitable operations, can be pushed aside before the strengths of the business can be explained to the bank by the owner. The business owner is not familiar with the terminology used by lenders. The bank's loan approval process is also unknown. The business owner does not know the major points that the lender is looking for.

The purpose of this guide is to make the loan request process easier for the business owner and improve the prospects of getting the financing that the business needs. The guide will help the owner identify the financial needs of the business and focus on the type of business loan(s) that should be considered. The guide will introduce concepts that are important to the bank in the loan approval process. Some of the concepts will already be familiar to the business owner. However, the financial analysis to be completed by the bank will seem like a foreign language. The objective of the business owner should be to present to the banker a concise and convincing presentation that will provide the necessary information about the business in a "lender-friendly" format. Bankers review numerous loan applications in their workweek and don't have the time to work through voluminous papers that are poorly organized and do not cover the main points that the banker is looking for.

The *Small-Business Loan Request Guide* will be a valuable resource that the business owner can refer to numerous times in the life of the business. The guide will provide insight into how the bank lender completes an assessment of the loan request and reaches a decision to approve or decline the request. It is written by a retired banker with over forty years of experience primarily spent in the small-business lending area. Utilization of the guide will provide valuable assistance and give the business owner confidence that he or she can be effective and successful in the process of seeking outside financing from a bank.

Business Summary

Lenders want to have a good idea who they will be doing business with. The following information will give the lender a snapshot of the business. It is important to provide this information in a complete and accurate fashion. Banks input information about their loan applicants into a management information system that allows them to track their lending activities. The information is also provided by the banks to their bank examiners in the federal or state governments. They are the following:

1. Legal form of the business (see explanations below)
2. Formation/origination date
3. Owners (and the ownership percentage of each owner)
4. Type of business (i.e., manufacturer, contractor, retailer, distributor, service business, automotive)
5. Brief description of products or services
6. Type of customers (consumers, businesses, government entities, nonprofit entities, exports)
7. Location(s) of the business

The primary legal forms of business are as follows:

1. Sole proprietorship
2. General partnership
3. Limited partnership
4. Limited liability company (LLC)
5. Corporation
6. S corporation

The business owners choose the legal form after consideration of several important issues. Each legal form will have an impact upon how businesses are taxed. The corporation is a distinct legal entity with profits taxed based upon corporate income tax rates. Any dividends paid to the owners are also taxed as personal income. This is commonly known as double taxation. All the other business entities (including the S corporation) do not pay an income tax. The owners are subject to a personal income tax based upon their share of the entity's reported profit. It also should be noted that the owners can report their share of the entity's reported loss on their personal tax returns. Such losses can offset income reported from other sources. The owners also select the business legal form to shield themselves from personal liabilities for any of the debts of the business and any claims against the business entity in a legal dispute. The owners are fully liable for such debts or claims in the case of a proprietorship and general partnership. In these cases, it is important that the business and/or the owners have liability insurance coverage. All the other business legal forms listed above allow the owners to not be personally liable for business debts or legal claims against the business. *Are you ready for the bad news?* All bank lenders (and other lenders such as leasing companies) normally require *personal guarantees* from the business owner(s) for loans or leases advanced to the business. The personal guarantees remove the personal liability protection provided by the legal form of the business and cause the owner(s) to be personally obligated to repay the business debt.

This guide will briefly mention that most banks use *credit scoring* as an important factor in the business loan approval process. Several service businesses provide to banks a numerical score (i.e., 160) based upon the model that they have developed to compute the score. The models of the service businesses are protected as proprietary information as the scoring providers do not want their models copied or duplicated by their competitors. The business formation date, type of business, length of time in business, and the personal credit scores of the owners are important components of the model. Financial information on the business is also a part of the computation of the score. Credit scoring can be a cause of anxiety for the business loan applicant. They are not familiar with how the score is computed. They also do not want to "roll the dice" and let credit scoring be an important factor in the financial future of the business. Lenders will argue that credit scoring allows their assessment of a loan application to be more objective. The business owner and loan applicant should concentrate upon completing the best presentation possible so that the bank lender can use the presentation in the decision-making process.

Loan Summary

LOAN PURPOSE AND BENEFITS

The loan applicant should provide a complete description of the loan request. The description should include the amount and type of loan (or loans) requested. The purpose of each loan and the benefit of each loan to the business should be carefully explained. The importance of this part of the application should not be ignored. The applicant demonstrates to the lender that he or she has knowledge of the business and its financial needs and has done some homework before approaching the lender. Loan requests that are poorly thought out and are unrealistic are usually declined before the lender reviews the business information provided.

Loan requests usually have the following purposes:

1. Purchases of equipment
2. Purchases of vehicles
3. Business real estate purchases
4. Business real estate improvements
5. Refinance existing business debts
6. Working capital for a specified period of time (see explanation below)
7. Working capital for the entire time period to follow (see explanation below)

Working Capital Loans

Working capital can be defined as funds that are available to cover operating expenses including purchases of inventory. Working capital funds may already be on hand, which allows the business to meet its expenses without the need to borrow from the bank. However, probably the most common loan request to a bank is to provide needed working capital to the business. Working capital loan requests can occur occasionally to purchase inventory for a large purchase order or to finance increased inventory to meet seasonal demand such as the holiday season. Working capital loan requests can also meet operating expenses when accounts receivable have increased due to a large purchase order, job, or contract. Cash that is needed in the business can be "tied up" in accounts receivable with bank borrowing required until the receivables are collected. Working capital loans also support seasonal businesses such as landscaping and contracting businesses (i.e., builders and electricians) that can have large jobs followed by a period of only a modest amount of work. These businesses have varied levels of revenues during the year and need to meet operating expenses when revenue levels are low. Working capital needs can also be more permanent and will continue in the following months of business operations. Increased working capital needs usually result from sales/revenue growth that requires increased inventory purchases, and also results in funds being tied up in higher levels of accounts receivable.

Loans to Finance Equipment, Vehicles, Real Estate, and Refinance Existing Debt

Equipment purchases can increase the productivity of the business and provide additional operating capabilities. The new equipment can also reduce operating costs, particularly in reduced repairs and maintenance expenses. If the benefits provided can be quantified, the numerical improvement in operating results is an important part of the applicant's financial presentation. New vehicle purchases can provide similar benefits to the business and can also expand the distribution capabilities of the business. Real estate purchase loans can enable the business to move to a better location and have improved facilities. The business may be nearing the end of its lease and can be vulnerable to significant increases in rent expense. Real estate improvement loans can also provide better facilities and also increase the efficiency of the business. Loans to refinance the existing debts of the business have the primary purpose of reducing the contractual payments required, causing an improvement in the cash flow of the business.

SOURCES AND USES OF FUNDS STATEMENT

Bank lenders will typically use the above statement to summarize the loan requests of the applicant. It is a good idea to be familiar with this statement. Presenting the loan request in the normal format of the statement will give the lender a good impression of the applicant's preparation. The statement is used when the applicant will be involved in a project, plan, or expansion, which will have multiple financing needs. In these cases, more than one type of loan may be requested, and other sources of funds may also be available to meet the financing needs. The example below is presented by a fictitious business, Coastal Landscaping LLC. This business will prepare examples of other statements in this guide, which will provide to the lender important presentations in the loan request package. In the *sources and uses of funds statement* below, Coastal Landscaping is requesting a $50,000 loan that will repay a family loan ($35,000), purchase tools ($10,000), and acquire a customer list ($5,000) of a nearby competitor, who is going out of business. Coastal Landscaping is also requesting a $50,000 line of credit to support working capital needs. The working capital needs of a landscaper consist of the need to cover operating expenses in the low-revenue winter months and the need to also pay operating expenses and nursery-plant purchases during the season. Landscapers who allow their customers to pay on credit terms will need the support of a working capital loan, which is normally structured as a line of credit. See further explanations below regarding a working capital line of credit.

Sources of Funds	*Uses of Funds*
$50,000—bank term loan	$35,000—repay family loan
$50,000—working capital loan	$10,000—tools
	$50,000—working capital for plants/materials, operating expenses
	$5,000—customer list
$100,000 *total sources*	$100,000 *total uses*

SUMMARY CHART OF LOAN TYPES

The following chart will give a summary of the different types of loans provided by bank lenders, and the normal repayment terms and security that they would usually require when extending the loan. The applicant should always have the business entity as the borrower on the loan request. Business assets and cash flow must be utilized to repay the loan. While the business owner will likely have to support the loan with a personal guarantee, it is desirable that business assets and cash flow be the source of repayment with no reliance upon personal assets. The lender will make the final decision regarding the loan amount, type of loan, and the terms. However, the applicant should be prepared to suggest the amount and type of loan that will benefit the business. It would be helpful for the applicant to be familiar with the chart below.

Type Loan	Purpose	Repayment Terms	Security
Line of credit	Working capital	One year, can be renewed annually	All business assets
Term loan	Equipment Property improvements	Three to seven years	All business assets Mortgage on property (property-improvement loans)
Term loan	Vehicles	Three to five years	Title to vehicle
Term loan	Refinance existing debt	Three to five years	All business assets
Term loan	Finance permanent increase in working capital to support growth	Three to five years	All business assets
Commercial mortgage	Purchase real estate	Fifteen to twenty years (see explanation for a balloon maturity below)	Mortgage on property
Letter of credit	Various (see below)	Usually one year	Bank certificate of deposit or all business assets

LOAN TERMS AND CONDITIONS

Bank lenders structure the term of a loan to match the useful life of the asset purchased from the loan proceeds. A loan to finance a new piece of equipment would be for a repayment term of five years. A larger piece of equipment such as a metal-working machine could be extended with a seven-year repayment term. The lender may decide that a used piece of equipment should only have a three-year repayment term. Both new and used vehicles can be normally financed over a five-year term. A line of credit is the best way to finance the ongoing working capital needs of the business. The borrower should make regular reductions to reduce the principal balance when cash flow improves. Regular reductions will create availability for future borrowings when cash flow becomes tighter. The bank will usually want to review the line of credit on an annual basis and approve continuing availability of the line of credit for another year after the review. The annual review will focus on whether the line of credit balance has been reduced on a regular basis. The bank will also review the financial condition and operating results of the business. The borrower will need to provide to the bank current financial statements and tax returns so that the bank can complete its review. See the section titled "A Good Presentation" at the end of this guide. A term loan may be approved at times to support a permanent increase in working capital that is necessary to support higher inventory and accounts receivable levels due to sales/revenue growth. When a bank initiates a borrowing relationship with a business, it expects to offer loans in the future to support working capital, equipment purchases, and other business financial needs. The bank will normally require a security interest in all business assets when the initial loan is made to obtain the collateral support of all the assets of the business. Vehicle loans will usually be secured by the vehicle purchased.

The acquisition of business real estate is financed by a mortgage with a long-term amortization of fifteen to twenty years. However, the bank often will structure the mortgage loan with a balloon maturity of five years. At the five year balloon maturity date, the balance of the loan is contractually due for full repayment. The bank will usually extend the maturity at the same rate of amortization if the loan is being paid as agreed and the financial condition and operating results of the business have not deteriorated. The balloon maturity date does allow the bank to revise the interest rate based upon prevailing interest rates at that time.

LETTERS OF CREDIT

A letter of credit is really not a loan involving the advancement of funds to the borrower. The letter of credit provides a guarantee of the bank to a third party that is doing business with the borrower, as required by a contract between the borrower and the third party. Terms of the letter of credit state that the third party may draw funds on the letter of credit if the borrower does not perform what is required by the contract between the parties. An example would be a contract to supply materials to the borrower over a given period. If the borrower does not remit payment to the third party as required by the contract, the third party can draw on the letter of credit to obtain the payment required. At that point, the borrower will owe the bank a loan equal to the amount of funds drawn. The unconditional guarantee provided by the bank often causes the bank to require a bank certificate of deposit (in the same amount as the letter of credit) to secure the letter of credit. The bank would want cash on hand to cover any draw on the letter of credit.

Letters of credit are also commonly used as a way of facilitating international trade. If the business exports or imports merchandise or goods, it should review with the bank the specific import or export transactions that will occur. Letters of credit are issued by the bank for the benefit of the foreign supplier to guarantee that the foreign supplier will be paid. An exporter can also have a letter of credit issued for its benefit to guarantee that the exporter will be paid by the foreign customer.

NEGOTIATING INTEREST RATES AND LOAN CONDITIONS

A small-business owner will find negotiating with the bank lender to be somewhat stressful. The cost of the loan consists of the interest rate and any fees to be charged to the borrower. The borrower will have less bargaining power on small loans (i.e., less than $250,000) as the bank is usually looking to achieve a rate of return mandated by management. Small loans generate less interest income than larger loans but often require the same amount of time to underwrite and process as a larger loan. The good news is that the borrower will benefit from competition between the banks in the community. A bank will not want to set pricing too high and risk losing market share in the small-business market.

Banks are *not* flexible in the areas of loan structure, which are listed as follows:

1. Security (also known as collateral)
2. Personal guarantees provided by business owners
3. Length of repayment term
4. Loan documents

Each bank has a written loan policy which indicates how each approved loan will be structured and documented. The purpose of the policy is to improve the quality of the bank's loan portfolio. Exceptions to policy are closely reviewed by bank management and are harshly discouraged. Small-business loan documents are produced by software packages purchased by the bank from an outside vendor. The documents are considered to be the only form that is acceptable for the small-business loan. Modifications are usually not permitted.

Business Description

A loan applicant will want to make sure that the lender understands the applicant's business operations, principal assets, products/services, customer base, marketing strategies, ownership, and management. The length of the previous sentence indicates that it will take time to fully explain to the lender all the above areas that are important to the business. It is desirable that the small-business owner(s) and the lender meet so that the lender can learn about the business. A number of items discussed in this section can be explained to the lender verbally. However, it is recommended that a written description be provided, covering the areas where the business has a unique strength. The business description should not be difficult to understand and should not be too technical.

The following categories should be explained to the lender:

1. SOURCES OF SALES/REVENUES

In this section, the applicant should provide information about the sources of sales/revenues. Lenders often use the terms *customer mix* and *product mix*. The customer mix consists of the customer names that make up the total revenues of the business. The product mix consists of the different types of products that make up the total revenues. The fictitious business in this guide, Coastal Landscaping LLC, has the following customer and product mixes:

Customer Mix

Various residential home owners	60%
ABC Apartment Complex	5%
DEF Apartment Complex	5%
Chesapeake Community Bank	10%
Crossroads Business Park	20%

Product Mix

Residential lawn mowing/maintenance	40%
Residential landscaping design/installation	20%
Apartment lawn mowing/maintenance	8%
Apartment snow removal	2%
Commercial lawn mowing/maintenance	17%
Commercial landscaping design/installation	10%
Commercial snow removal	3%

The above listing will indicate the applicant's target market. The applicant should indicate who the competitors are in the market area and how the business is unique and superior when compared to the competition. The term *niche* is often used in small-business marketing plans. A niche is a portion of the market that would benefit from the products or services offered by the business, and no other competitor is currently selling to this market. The niche is a grouping of potential customers where the applicant can be the dominant business.

The applicant should explain the reasons for the current trend in the level of total sales/revenues and refer to trends in the customer mix and product mix in the explanation. Another important issue to the lender is whether there is a considerable concentration of customers in the customer mix. If any one customer name represents 20% or more of the total of revenues, there is a risk to the applicant if this customer is lost to the competition. The history and current status of the customer relationship should be explained to the lender. In the case of Coastal Landscaping LLC, the customer relationship with Crossroads Business Park should be explained.

2. BUSINESS LOCATION

Describe the facilities of the business and the business location(s). The geographic location and specific business location are extremely important if the business is a retailer. A critical consideration is where the customer base is located and their proximity to where the business is located. Where does the customer purchase occur? How is the product or service distributed or delivered to the customer? Local business / economic conditions have an important impact on the performance of the business. The applicant should provide a brief summary of how local business and economic conditions affect their business. Indicate if the location(s) are owned or leased, and the lease or mortgage terms.

3. KEY SOURCES OF SUPPLY

Sources of supply are of great importance to retailers and businesses that purchase a large quantity of products or materials, such as contractors, distributors, and manufacturers. The applicant should mention the primary suppliers to the business and whether alternative suppliers are available to the business. Indicate the materials supplied and recent trends in costs. Formal legal contracts with suppliers should also be described. Credit terms provided by the supplier to the applicant (i.e., thirty days from the invoice date) should be indicated in the presentation. Is the applicant a member of any buying group that provides the benefit of reduced prices? Does the business utilize subcontractors? Frequent users of subcontractors are manufacturers and contractors.

4. BUSINESS OPERATIONS AND MAJOR PIECES OF EQUIPMENT

Briefly describe how the business operates in order to produce or distribute its product or service. The explanation should not be overly technical. List the major pieces of equipment that are utilized in business operations. Is this equipment owned or leased? What is the impact of technology on the business? It is important for the applicant to realize that extravagant purchases of equipment, furniture, or improvements to the business property are an unwise use of business funds. Given the funding limitations of every small business, capital purchases must have a positive impact upon revenues and profits.

5. Intangible Assets

Intangible assets are assets of the business that are not considered physical assets, such as real estate, equipment, and inventory. It is difficult to determine a specific value of the intangible assets listed below. There is no acquisition cost that can be identified. However, intangible assets can be the most important assets of the business and the primary reason that the business is successful. The applicant should list any of the assets listed below that are important to the business and give an explanation so that the lender can understand why the intangible asset is considered valuable:

a. Patents
b. Brand name
c. Unique and positive business reputation in the market place
d. Logos/trademarks
e. Franchise
f. Technical expertise
g. License
h. Customer list
i. Owner reputation in the market

6. How Are Products/Services Marketed and Distributed to the Customer Base?

The applicant should explain how the product or service is sold to the customer. *Marketing* is a term that describes how the business communicates the benefits of its products/services to the potential customer and influences the customer to make a decision to purchase. The business must also make it convenient for the customer to make the purchase. The place of purchase may be a retail store, the business location of the customer, a telephone order, or the website of the business. Indicate how the product or service is distributed or delivered to the customer. The geographic area of the target market should also be explained. The marketing effort can be performed in the following ways after the business identifies the target customer and determines the best communication method. The wrong method will cause the business to fall short of its revenue goal. Marketing methods include the following:

a. Personal selling by the owner and/or sales personnel
b. Independent representatives, distributors, or retailers
c. A website
d. A catalogue followed by orders over the phone
e. Direct mailing of a brochure, sales letter, or flyer
f. Telemarketing
g. Trade shows

The applicant should also describe the pricing strategy of the business and how the pricing strategy compares with the competition. If credit terms are offered to the customer, indicate the payment terms (i.e., thirty days from the date of the invoice).

7. OWNERS AND KEY EMPLOYEES

The applicant should list each owner and give a brief explanation of the roles and responsibilities of that owner in the business. It would also be helpful to mention any special skills and/or accomplishments of the owner. The listing should also include any nonowners who are considered key employees. The key employees would have valuable skills in operations, marketing, or finance. A personal resume could also be included as an attachment if presentation of the resume is considered an important item in the loan request package. The ownership and management team is, without a doubt, the most important asset of a small business. Effective presentation of this asset is essential in the loan presentation.

The following items should also be mentioned to the lender:

a. Does the business have a key-person life insurance policy on any of the individuals mentioned above?
b. Are any of the employees union members? What is the status of the labor agreement?

8. PROFESSIONALS AND ADVISORS

Indicate the professionals that service the business, such as the accountant, lawyer, and insurance agent. These names are important to the lender. Banks maintain listings of professionals that are used by their small-business customers. The bank's objective is to have good working relationships with professionals, and they often benefit from referrals that are the source of new banking relationships. It is also beneficial to the loan applicant if they use a professional that has a good relationship with the bank. The loan presentation should also include the following:

a. A listing of the forms of business insurance carried by the applicant.
b. A description of the types of financial information prepared by the accountant (i.e., tax returns, compilation financial statements).
c. Is the business or any of the owners involved in a lawsuit or any other legal action?

Income Statement Analysis

The time to work with numbers has arrived! Small-business owners prefer to concentrate upon operating their businesses and selling their products or services to their customers. The owner(s) have interests and skills that have provided the foundation of the business and also have defined its purpose. Maintaining and analyzing financial records is often considered a less desirable use of time. *However,* "reading the numbers" will always be a key part of the successful management of a small business. If financial information is not reviewed on a regular basis, the business owner is traveling to a destination without knowing what road he or she is on. Understanding the performance and needs of the business requires looking at the numbers and understanding how they relate to each other.

One method of analysis is preparing and reviewing spreadsheets, which consist of financial statements that are spread side by side to facilitate comparisons. This guide will use spreadsheets often to evaluate the operating performance and financial condition of a business. Computer software products are available to allow spreadsheet analysis to occur without difficulty. Financial analysis using spreadsheets may seem to be arduous, but it is the best way to spot trends and changes in the financial picture.

Income statement spreads for Coastal Landscaping LLC are presented below:

	2011—Actual	2012—Actual	2013—Projected
Lawn maintenance	$67,733	$94,080	$96,000
Plants, shrubs	$0	$14,000	$44,000
Snowplowing	$12,000	$5,000	$8,000
Total revenues	$79,733	$113,080	$148,000
Production salaries	$11,433	$22,200	$28,000
Cost of plants, shrubs	$0	$5,388	$17,600
Other direct costs	$9,500	$10,393	$15,000
(fuel, supplies, maintenance)			
Total variable costs	$20,933	$37,981	$60,600
Gross profit	$58,800	$75,099	$87,400
Gross profit margin	73.7%	66.4%	59.1%
Other expenses	$11,300	$12,274	$12,400
Interest expense	$1,500	$1,200	$5,000
Owner's salary	$36,000	$38,000	$40,000
Operating profit	$10,000	$23,625	$30,000

Note: Depreciation expense is not included because it is not an expenditure of cash.

GROSS PROFIT AND GROSS PROFIT MARGIN

Gross profit is defined as revenues minus variable expenses. Variable expenses are directly related to the revenues that are generated by the business. When revenues are in a growth mode, variable expenses will also increase. When revenues are declining, the level of variable expenses will decrease. The gross profit margin is a percentage consisting of the gross profit divided by revenues. Many small-business owners view the success of the business by only looking at the level of sales/revenues. This is sometimes referred to as the "sales mentality." The gross profit and gross profit margin are better indicators of the success of the business. A business is viable if a sufficient level of gross profit is earned to cover fixed expenses (discussed below) and earn a profit.

The income statement on the previous page indicates an interesting trend for Coastal Landscaping LLC. Revenues are showing strong growth. The growth in revenues has allowed gross profits to also increase, but the gross profit margin is declining. The small-business owner can make an assessment of this trend by looking at each of the products of the business and evaluating the trend in revenues, gross profits, and gross profit margins for each product. The operating results for the business indicate the following:

	Lawn Maintenance		Plants/Shrubs		Snowplowing	
2011						
Revenues	$67,733		$0		$12,000	
Production salaries	$11,433	16.9%	$0		$0	
					(owner does the plowing)	
Cost of plants/shrubs	$0		$0		$0	
Other direct costs	$5,500	8.1%	$0		$4,000	33.0%
Gross profit	$50,800	75.0%	$0		$8,000	67.0%
2012						
Revenues	$94,080		$14,000		$5,000	
Production salaries	$18,000	19.1%	$4,200	30.0%	$0	
Cost of plants/shrubs	$0		$5,388	38.4%	$0	
Other direct costs	$6,743	7.1%	$2,000	14.3%	$1,650	33.0%
Gross profit	$69,337	73.8%	$2,412	17.3%	$3,350	67.0%
2013—Projected						
Revenues	$96,000		$44,000		$8,000	
Production salaries	$19,200	20.0%	$8,800	20.0%	$0	
Cost of plants/shrubs	$0		$17,600	40.0%	$0	
Other direct costs	$8,000	8.3%	$4,000	9.0%	$3,000	37.5%
Gross profit	$68,800	71.7%	$13,600	31.0%	$5,000	62.5%

The product analysis indicates that the primary business of lawn maintenance has shown growth with a gross profit margin that is projected to decline slightly due to higher fuel costs and a modest increase in production salaries paid to part-time seasonal workers. As indicated on page 27, the projected gross profit margin for the entire business of Coastal Landscaping LLC is projected to decline from 73.7% in 2011 to a projected 59.1% in 2013. The decline in GPM is attributed to the change in the *product mix* of the business. The acquisition of the commercial accounts of Chesapeake Community Bank and Crossroads Business Park in 2011 led the business into providing landscape design services to include planting small trees, plants, and shrubs on the grounds. Revenues in this product category will increase in 2013 from the modest level earned in 2012. This new product offering of the business earns a gross profit margin that is lower than the primary lawn-maintenance business. However, the gross profits earned in landscaping design and installation will provide a good supplement to the lawn-maintenance business and help generate an increase in total gross profits. The risk to the business is a decline in the GPM of landscaping design/installation due to errors in job bidding, and the possible reduction in time devoted to the primary lawn-maintenance business, which has a higher GPM. This case indicates the importance of a regular review of the financial data in the operation of the business to assess the profitability of each product or service. Software available for sale at business office supply stores provides the capability to generate financial statements as often as monthly. The review of monthly financial information is a fundamental part of effective financial management.

FIXED EXPENSES

Fixed expenses are not as difficult to project as sales/revenues and variable expenses. Fixed expenses will usually remain the same while the level of sales/revenues will vary. The small-business owner should address fixed expenses with a line-by-line budgeting approach. Salaries are usually the most important line item in the budgeting process. As noted above, landscaping production salaries are considered variable expenses as they consist of salaries paid to part-time seasonal workers. However, production salaries can also have the characteristic of a fixed expense if production workers consist of full-time employees. The recent recession caused a considerable decline in small-business revenues. Reducing salary expenses was the most effective way to avoid considerable operating losses. However, terminating an employee that has been a good contributor to the business is a very difficult decision, which is often postponed for a significant period of time.

Owner Compensation

The compensation of the owners in the form of salaries, distributions, and dividends is also a critically important fixed expense of a small business. The level of compensation is determined by personal factors such as living expenses and annual personal loan payment obligations (i.e., mortgage, auto loan, credit cards). It is important that the compensation of the owners does not deplete the cash and working capital position of the business. When the business is in the early stages of operations, other personal income such as a spouse's salary can reduce the need to draw income from the new business. Other income can also be a help in a period of declining sales, low profits, or an operating loss. The method of taxation also has an impact on the level of owner compensation. If the business is an S corporation, partnership, LLC, or a proprietorship, the business profits are included in the taxable income of the owner(s). The owner(s) need to draw from the business sufficient funds to cover the personal tax liability.

Breakeven Analysis

Breakeven analysis is useful to businesses in the very early stage of operations as the owner(s) want to determine the level of sales/revenues that will cover operating expenses and annual loan repayment obligations. The analysis is also helpful to businesses currently operating at a loss as the owner(s) plan to improve their operating results and profitability. The variables needed to compute the breakeven level of sales/revenues are as follows:

1. Gross profit margin
2. Fixed operating expenses (excluding depreciation and interest)
3. Annual required principal and interest payments on business debt

The calculation for Coastal Landscaping LLC is as follows:

Fixed operating expenses (defined above) *plus* annual loan repayment *Divided by* the gross profit margin

Based upon the 2013 projection on page 27,

$52,400 *plus* $19,860 (see debt schedule on page 38) *divided by* 0.591 *equals* $122,267—breakeven sales/revenues

Projected sales/revenues in 2013 totaling $148,000 exceed breakeven sales/revenues totaling $122,267. There is not a lot of margin for error in the operation of the business. This is typical of all small businesses, which usually have thin profit margins. It should be noted that any further decline in the GPM will increase the level of breakeven sales/revenues. In the case of Coastal Landscaping LLC, the breakeven level of sales/revenues will increase if the lower-margin landscaping/ design (plants and shrubs) portion of the business continues to make up a larger percentage of total sales/revenues.

Cash Flow Analysis

SALES AND PROFITS ARE *NOT* CASH FLOW

The owner of a small business such as Coastal Landscaping LLC may look at the profits earned by the business as indicated on page 27 and feel comfortable that all bills and operating expenses can be paid on time without difficulty. That is a *wrong* assumption. There are a number of factors that affect the cash flow of the business. These factors are not revealed on an annual income statement such as the income statements shown on page 27. Businesses such as landscaping can be seasonal businesses when revenues vary considerably during the year from high points to very low points. When revenues are at a low point, the cash flow of the business is usually at a deficit. Businesses that allow their customers to pay on credit terms must consider how long it takes the customer to pay the invoice and whether the customer is creditworthy, with the risk that it may not even make a partial payment. Businesses such as retailers need to address how long it takes to sell the inventory that they have purchased and whether they will have sufficient cash to pay the supplier. The supplier may be offering thirty-day terms or may be requiring cash on delivery, especially for new businesses.

CASH FLOW OF COASTAL LANDSCAPING LLC

An income statement alone will not show how cash flows into and out of the business. A separate financial statement showing cash flow would reflect the deposits to the business checking account and the checks issued from the account. A month-to-month cash flow statement would show how revenues and accounts receivable collections will vary in amount during the year. Operating expenses will also change in amount each month as indicated by the amount and quantity of checks issued. The following cash flow projection for Coastal Landscaping LLC is based upon the income statement projection for 2013 on page 27. The cash flow projection should be prepared after the income statement projection. The cash flow projection is presented on a monthly basis, reflecting the initial six months of the year.

	Jan.	Feb.	Mar.	Apr.	May	June
Snowplowing	$3,500	$3,500	$1,000	$0	$0	$0
Lawn mainten.	$0	$0	$0	$0	$13,700	$13,700
Plants/shrubs	$0	$0	$0	$0	$3,000	$5,000
Total cash in	$3,500	$3,500	$1,000	$0	$16,700	$18,700
Production salaries	$0	$0	$0	$3,340	$3,740	$5,940
Plants/shrubs cost	$0	$0	$0	$1,200	$2,000	$6,400
Other direct costs	$1,320	$1,320	$360	$1,714	$1,714	$1,714
Insurance expense	$1,200	$0	$0	$0	$0	$0
Officer salary	$3,300	$3,300	$3,300	$3,300	$3,300	$3,300
Other expenses	$1,334	$1,334	$1,084	$884	$884	$884
Loan payments	$560	$560	$1,655	$1,655	$1,655	$1,655
Total cash out	$7,714	$6,514	$6,399	$12,093	$13,293	$19,893
Surplus (defic.)	($4,214)	($3,014)	($5,399)	($12,093)	$3,407	($1,193)
Cumulative surplus (defic.)	($4,214)	($7,228)	($12,627)	($24,720)	($21,313)	($22,506)
Line of credit			up to $25,000 borrowed by the end of April			

The most significant factor affecting the cash flow of the landscaping business is its seasonality. Only a nominal amount of revenues are generated in the winter months from snow plowing at commercial properties. Coastal Landscaping LLC will need to borrow at least $25,000 on the requested line of credit to cover the shortfall in cash flow from January to the end of April. The lawn care and landscaping business began to generate revenues in April. However, the thirty-day credit terms that are offered to the customers delay the receipt of cash until May. Another factor affecting cash flow is the fact that the plants/shrubs nursery supplier requires payment in cash when the items are taken from the nursery to the landscaping job site. Cash spent for plants/shrubs occurs one month before the customer pays the invoice for installation of the nursery products.

OPERATING CYCLE OF THE BUSINESS

The monthly statement of cash flow above indicates the impact that changes in revenue levels have on the cash flow and cash position of the business. The operating cycle will also be an important factor in the cash flow of the business, especially in businesses that have inventories for sale (i.e., retailers and suppliers). The operating cycle analyzes the accounts receivable collection period and the level of inventory, which is measured as days of sales on hand. The payment terms offered by the suppliers of inventory (i.e., thirty days from invoice date) are also a part of the analysis. The accounts receivable collection period and inventory on hand (measured as days of sales on hand) can be calculated from the financial statements of the business as follows:

Accounts Receivable Collection Period	*Days of Inventory on Hand*
Revenues *divided* by days in the period (i.e., 365) *equals* revenues per day	Cost of sales *divided* by days in the period *equals* inventory sold per day
Accounts receivable at the statement date *divided* by revenues per day *equals* the collection period	Inventory at the statement date *divided* by inventory sold per day *equals* inventory days on hand

The following compares the operating cycle of Coastal Landscaping LLC to a supplier of building materials to builders/contractors:

	Coastal Landscaping	*Building Materials Supplier*
Accts. receiv. collection period	30 days (same as credit terms offered to customers)	50 days (builders can be slow pay)
Inventory on hand in days	zero (no inventory carried as inventory is delivered to the job site)	90 days
Total operating cycle	30 days	140 days
Less: Accts. payable terms	0 days (nursery suppliers require cash at pickup)	(30 days)
Financing support needed	30 days	110 days

A cash flow projection similar to the one above would indicate the size of the line of credit needed by the business. However, the above analysis is also useful and suggests that the longer operating cycle of the building materials supplier will require a larger line of credit than the landscaper. The following financial information will give the business owner a more exact report of the status of accounts receivable, inventory, and accounts payable. This information is vital to the effective management of the cash flow of the business.

INVENTORY LEVELS

Computer software can provide regular reports of the inventory of the business. The business owner should monitor the inventory levels as often as monthly. The cash flow of the business will improve with effective management of this asset. Slow-moving items should be identified with selling prices marked down and future purchases reduced. The owner should work closely with suppliers with the objective of ordering lower quantities more frequently. This is known as "just in time" inventory management.

ACCOUNTS RECEIVABLE AGING

Computer software can provide a listing of all customers who have outstanding accounts with the business. The aging should be reviewed and updated on a regular basis to determine which customers should be contacted regarding late payments. Remember the saying, "The squeaky wheel gets the grease." An aging format is as follows, and a current aging should be presented to the bank with the loan application:

Account Name   Balance Owed   Invoice Date   Days from Invoice Date

ACCOUNTS PAYABLE AGING

Computer software can also provide a listing of all suppliers who are presently owed unpaid invoices. The aging should also be reviewed and updated on a regular basis. Good relationships with suppliers are critical to the business. All accounts should be paid by the due date. If for some reason a payment will be late, the supplier should be contacted and advised about the situation. Discounts should be taken whenever possible. If discounts are not available, the payment should be remitted a short time before the due date. An aging format is as follows, and a current aging should be presented to the bank with the loan application:

Supplier Name   Balance Owed   Invoice Date   Days from Invoice Date

CASH FLOW OF A BUILDER/CONTRACTOR
USE OF A JOBS-IN-PROCESS SCHEDULE

Builders/contractors are frequent users of a line of credit offered by banks. A tight or negative cash position can occur during a period when the level of jobs in process is high. Labor must be paid weekly or biweekly. Material suppliers may want to be paid cash on delivery or preferably on thirty-day terms. The above direct costs on a job must be paid in cash before contract billings to the customer / property owner are paid. Often the customer will take as long as sixty to ninety days to pay a billing as they want to inspect the work that is being done. A builder/contractor should prepare and submit to the bank a *jobs-in-process schedule,* which should contain the information shown in the following schedule. The builder/contactor should also prepare and review frequently *accounts receivable* and *accounts payable agings* indicating the information noted above. The above statements provide needed information to the builder/contractor about the profitability and cash flow of their jobs in process.

Jobs-in-Process Schedule

	Contract Name	*Contract Name*	*Contract Name*
Contact amount			
Direct labor and material costs			
Contract gross profit			
Contract billings to date			
Direct contract costs to date			
Projected completion date			

CASH FLOW GENERATED FROM BUSINESS OPERATIONS (A LENDER'S ANALYSIS)

Lenders often use a simpler measurement of business cash flow that is taken entirely from the income statement. The calculation is *net profit + depreciation + interest.* Depreciation is added to net profit because it is an expense that does not involve the expenditure of cash. Interest expense is added to net profit as lenders want to compare the sum of NP + depreciation + interest to all principal and interest payments due on the debt of the business. The following lists the business cash flow for Coastal Landscaping LLC using this simpler measurement.

	Actual 2012	*Projected 2013*
Net profit + deprec. + interest	$24,825	$35,000

A *debt schedule* using the format below should be prepared for the lender so that the comparison between business cash flow and loan payments can be completed. The following is a debt schedule prepared by Coastal Landscaping LLC:

Lender	Original Amount	Present Balance	Monthly Payment	Security
Ford credit	$15,000	$9,000	$300	Truck
Ford credit	$13,000	$7,000	$260	Truck
Requested term loan	$50,000 after settlement	$50,000	$980	Business assets
Requested line of credit	$50,000	draws to follow	$115 (interest only at 50% usage)	Business assets

Total monthly payment: $1,655

Total annual payments: $19,860

A lender will calculate a ratio known as *debt service coverage*. The ratio compares the business cash flow (net profit + depreciation + interest) to the projected annual principal and interest payments on the debt listed in the debt schedule. Two ratios are usually calculated. One ratio shows the coverage provided by the last year of actual operations (2012), and the other ratio shows the coverage provided by projected cash flow.

	Actual 2012	Projected 2013
Net profit + deprec. + interest	$24,825	$35,000
Projected annual loan payments	($19,860)	($19,860)
Excess cash flow	$4,965	$15,140
Debt coverage ratio	1.25×	1.76×

The debt service coverage ratios show adequate coverage of projected loan payments. However, lenders will ask additional questions about *other planned expenditures / uses of funds,* which will not appear on the income statement. These expenditures or uses of funds may or may not be covered by the *excess cash flow* shown above in the debt coverage presentation.

Other Planned Expenditures / Uses of Funds

1. *Distributions to owners in addition to their salary.* Distributions are needed to pay income taxes resulting from the reporting of business profits on the personal tax return.

2. *Capital expenditures.* The lender will ask about planned expenditures for equipment and property improvements. They will want to know what amount will be funded by loans with the balance funded by business cash flow or an additional equity investment of the owner(s).

3. *Retention of funds to increase working capital and support growth.* See the discussion of working capital in the next section. The business should retain funds to increase its working capital position if sales/revenues are trending higher.

If the excess cash flow as computed above in the debt service coverage is not sufficient to cover the other planned expenditures / uses of funds, the cash flow of the business must be supplemented by another source of funds. The bank lender will need an explanation regarding this other source of funds, which could be additional capital provided by the owner(s) and/or an additional borrowing from the bank.

Balance Sheet Analysis

A balance sheet is a snapshot of the financial condition of a business at a specific point in time. A balance sheet is usually prepared as of the final day of the period that the income statement covers. The composition of the balance sheet is the result of the following factors:

1. The cost of the assets purchased
2. The amount of debt and other liabilities of the business
3. The amount of equity invested by the business owners
4. The cash flow of the business up to the balance sheet date

The actual December 31, 2012, balance sheet of Coastal Landscaping LLC is presented below along with the projected June 30, 2013, balance sheet.

	Actual 12/31/12	*Projected 06/30/13*	
Cash	$10,000	$12,214	
Accounts receivable	$0	$30,000	(30-day terms are offered)
Inventory	$0	$0	(inventory is delivered directly to the job site)
Total current assets	$10,000	$42,214	
Trucks and trailers	$30,000	$26,000	
Mowers, tools, and equip.	$20,000	$30,000	($10,000 purchased with term loan)
Customer list	$0	$5,000	(purchased with the term loan)
Goodwill	$10,000	$10,000	(value of business name purchased in 2010)
Total assets	$70,000	$113,214	
Accounts payable	$1,000	$1,000	
Line of credit borrowings	$0	$25,000	
Total current liabilities	$1,000	$26,000	
Truck loans	$16,000	$13,300	
Family loan	$35,000	$0	(repaid by term loan)
Bank term loan	$0	$47,200	($50,000 advanced in March)
Total liabilities	$52,000	$86,500	
Net worth	$18,000	$26,714	
Total liabs. and NW	$70,000	$113,214	
Working capital	$9,000	$16,214	(current assets minus current liabs.)
Current ratio	10.0×	1.62×	(current assets / current liabs.)
Total liabs. / net worth	2.89×	3.24×	

Projected balance sheets are not usually prepared as a part of the loan application. However, the preparation of a projected balance sheet is informative if the financial condition of the business is going to change significantly. In the case of Coastal Landscaping LLC, the seasonality of the business causes the off-season balance sheet in the winter to be far different from the in-season balance sheet in the summer. When reviewing a balance sheet of a business, bank lenders focus on two factors that provide the best indication of the financial condition of a business: *working capital* and *owner equity* or *capital invested.*

WORKING CAPITAL

Current assets will most likely turn to cash within twelve months of the balance sheet date while current liabilities will most likely need to be paid within twelve months of the balance sheet date. If the current ratio (current assets divided by current liabilities) is less than 1×, the financial condition of the business is weak and needs the immediate attention of the owners(s). The focus should return to the cash flow and profitability of the business as discussed in the previous sections. Can revenues be increased and collected in a shorter time period? Can expenses be reduced without a negative impact on the operation of the business? Can the profitability of the business be improved? Can the debt of the business be restructured to reduce the monthly contractual payments? Can expenditures for new equipment be postponed?

As of June 30, 2013, the projected current ratio of Coastal Landscaping LLC is satisfactory at 1.62×. Cash plus accounts receivable of $42,214 covers total current liabilities of $26,000. The business is able to gain a liquidity position that covers the line of credit borrowings, which supported the weak cash flow period in the winter and early spring. Cash flow in the remaining months of the lawn-care/landscaping season should be sufficient to reduce line of credit borrowings to zero by October.

OWNER EQUITY OR CAPITAL INVESTED

There is one characteristic that is common for all small businesses. Capital is a limited source of funds to support the business. Lenders like to see invested owner equity not less than 20% of the total assets of a business. That would mean that total liabilities should not be greater than 4× the amount of owner equity (a.k.a. net worth). The balance sheet of Coastal Landscaping LLC as of December 31, 2012, is typical of a small business with a limited capital source. Prior to 2010, the business was very small, consisting of residential lawn-mowing accounts with a modest amount of invested capital. In 2010, the assets and business name of a competitor were purchased which significantly increased the assets and revenues of the business. A loan from the family in the amount of $35,000 funded the business purchase. The requested loan of $50,000 will pay off in full the family loan. The projected balance sheet as of June 30, 2013, indicates a ratio of total liabilities / net worth of 3.24×. The new $50,000 loan and borrowings under the line of credit totaling $25,000 cause the ratio to be at a high point as of June 30, 2013. In the final months of the lawn-maintenance/landscaping season, the line of credit borrowings will be reduced to zero from the seasonal cash flow. The lower level of outstanding debt and retention of the business profits will reduce the total liabilities / net worth ratio in the fall.

Collateral, Personal Guarantees, and Legal Agreements

This section will move away from financial analysis and will cover other important factors in the lender's approval of the loan. Collateral and personal guarantees are considered in the approval decision and are a part of the loan structure. The lender will also need to be aware of any other legal agreements which the business is obligated to comply with as they may have an impact on the approval decision.

COLLATERAL SCHEDULE

The collateral for the loan is ultimately the lender's decision. The business owner should list in the loan presentation the assets that are available to secure the loan. The listing should be in the following format:

Business Assets

Description	Balance sheet amount or amount on aging or schedule	Cost (if asset is being purchased from the loan proceeds)
Accounts receivable		
Inventory		
Existing equipment		
Equipment being purchased		
Existing vehicles		
Vehicles being purchased		

Real Estate Assets

Owner	Location	Approx. value	Amt. of prior mortgage liens and repayment terms

Collateral is an important part of the loan approval. If weaknesses occur in the profitability and cash flow of the business, the collateral provides to the lender a second or backup source of repayment. The applicant should provide sufficient description of each asset available as collateral and include additional information such as a current accounts receivable aging and a listing of the larger pieces of equipment (i.e., equipment with an estimated value in excess of $10,000). Bank lenders are very conservative concerning the estimated value of the collateral offered by the applicant. If a business defaults on its loan, its assets have usually been reduced to a significantly lower value. If the business is forced to sell or liquidate the assets in the used market, only nominal values can be expected in the effort to reduce the principal amount of the loan from the sale of collateral. The following listing gives an estimate of the discounted values assigned by the bank to the types of collateral. The discounting of values occurs in the bank's review of the loan prior to approval. It should be noted that the discounted values will most likely not be obtained if the business is forced to liquidate its assets. The applicant should be aware of the reason for the bank's conservative view of collateral values.

Asset Type	Lower Value after the Discount
Accounts receivable	70% to 80% of amount on the balance sheet or aging
Inventory	33% to 50% of amount on the balance sheet
New equipment	80% of purchase price
Used equipment	60% of purchase price
New vehicles	85% of purchase price
Used vehicles	75% of purchase price
Business real estate	75% to 80% of appraised value

PERSONAL GUARANTEES

The bank will normally require the personal guarantee of any owner with a 20% or more ownership interest in the business. Each owner will be asked to complete a personal financial statement on the bank's form and provide copies of the last two personal tax returns that were filed. The lender's review of the personal statement and tax returns will focus on the following areas:

1. Personal liquid assets consisting of cash and marketable securities. Personal liquidity is important as it indicates the owner's ability to advance cash to the business if the cash position of the business becomes tight.
2. The value of the personal residence and other real estate owned, including the existing mortgage liens on the property. (It should be noted that the lender *may require* a mortgage lien on the personal real estate to secure the business loan if the lender's

evaluation of the business-asset collateral falls short of the value needed to secure the requested loan.)
3. The schedule of personal indebtedness contained in the personal financial statement.
4. Other sources of personal income which are separate from the business.

LEGAL AGREEMENTS

The applicant should list all other legal agreements that are obligations of the business. Such agreements would include the following:

1. Real estate leases.
2. Equipment leases.
3. Loan agreements of other lenders.
4. Franchise agreement.
5. Noncompete agreement.
6. Buy-sell agreements between the owners.
7. Contracts to build or improve real estate (applies to contractors). Indicate the contract amount, projected job profit, and completion date.
8. Contracts with suppliers.
9. Union contracts.

The applicant should also explain any lawsuits currently in process in which the business or any of its owners are a party.

SBA Program Loans

Banks can make loans to small businesses with the support of a guaranty by the Small Business Administration (an agency of the federal government). The guaranty does not cover 100% of the loan amount, but it covers a significant portion of the loan to allow the bank to approve and fund a loan it would otherwise decline. Situations that are candidates for an SBA-guaranteed loan are as follows:

1. The collateral coverage of the loan amount falls short of bank guidelines or policy.
2. The business has been operating for a short time. It has yet to show two to three years of profitable operations.
3. The business is requesting a loan to support the cost of a significant expansion (a larger business property, new equipment, the introduction of a new product, or the purchase of another business).
4. The business is recovering from a prior period of operating losses.
5. The business is a start-up (see the next section).

Bank Lenders Participating in the SBA Program

It is important to know if the bank that will review the loan application participates in the SBA program. The highest level of participation is the *preferred lender status*. Banks that have obtained this status have a proven history of making SBA-guaranteed loans. Preferred lender banks actually approve the loan (and not the SBA).

The bank must follow the SBA lending policies and guidelines. The bank's approval significantly reduces the turnaround time from the initial request to the final approval and funding of the loan. Banks that do not have the preferred lender status can also make SBA-guaranteed loans. However, the SBA needs to review and approve the application package. Some banks choose not to make SBA-guaranteed loans as the process can be very cumbersome and time-consuming if the bank's lenders are not familiar with the process.

If the bank determines that the loan request should be supported with an SBA guaranty, work closely with the bank lender to provide the necessary information. The bank will have an application form that is used specifically for an SBA-guaranteed loan. This guide covers the information about the business and the owners that is typically required in an SBA loan application. Use this guide in the preparation of an SBA application.

COLLATERAL, GUARANTEES, AND LOAN STRUCTURE

As noted above, an SBA-guaranteed loan is often the alternative to a loan request that is declined by the bank due to a shortfall in collateral coverage or other weaknesses. However, the SBA-guaranteed loan will usually be secured by all business assets *and* mortgages on the personal residences of the owner(s). An SBA-guaranteed loan to purchase real estate can be advanced in an amount up to 90% of the value of the business property. The business property purchased must be at least 51% occupied by the business applicant. Any owner with an ownership interest of 20% or more in the business will be required to support the loan with a personal guarantee.

SBA-guaranteed loans make available to the borrower longer repayment terms than conventional bank business loans. Given the longer repayment terms, an SBA-guaranteed loan is an important source of capital for the business. Maximum repayment terms are as follows:

1. Working capital loans—5 to 10 years
2. Equipment loans—up to 10 years
3. Real estate loans—up to 25 years

Loans to Start-Up Businesses

This is the most challenging section of this guide. It covers the most difficult loan to get approved at a bank—a loan to finance the start-up of a business. A bank will only fund a start-up loan on an exception basis. An SBA-guaranteed loan is probably the most likely external source of funding available to a start-up entrepreneur. The most important factors evaluated by a lender in a start-up business loan are as follows:

1. Start-up costs should be listed in detail with the probability that the costs are usually higher than expected. Listed on the next page are start-up costs for Coastal Landscaping LLC under the assumption that the business will begin operations on December 31, 2012.
2. A conservative income statement projection should be prepared along with the cash flow projection noted below. The assumptions should be well thought out and explained in the loan presentation. Refer to the *business description* and *income statement analysis* sections of this guide to determine the content of the assumptions. The income statement projection format should show revenues and expenses on a monthly basis for the first year of operations. The second year of projected operations can be presented on an annual basis without the separate monthly columns.
3. A conservative cash flow projection should be prepared to determine how much the business's start-up cash balance should be. A margin for error should always be factored into

the beginning cash balance amount. A start-up business will usually have losses and negative cash flow for a considerable period after the doors are opened. The cash flow projection should be presented on a monthly basis for the first year of operations.

4. The cash investment of the owners should be enough to avoid a start-up that is entirely funded with debt. A guideline would be an equity investment not less than 20% of total start-up costs. A personal financial statement of each owner should be presented to show the personal liquid assets available to invest in the business. Each owner should retain sufficient personal liquid assets to meet living expenses, personal debt payments, and have a reserve for unexpected situations and emergencies.

5. The projected cash flow of the business needs to be at a sufficient level to cover the monthly payments on the loan requested. As noted above, the projection should be conservative.

START-UP COSTS FOR COASTAL LANDSCAPING LLC (START-UP DATE OF DECEMBER 31, 2012)

Start-up cash balance	$40,000
Start-up marketing expense	$2,500
Professional fees	$2,000
First month of rent	$250
Supplies	$400
Trucks and trailers	$30,000
Mowers, tools, and equipment	$20,000
Business name purchased	$10,000
Total	$105,150

Loans to Finance Residential Investment Properties

This guide will consider the rental of residential properties a small business. Banks receive numerous requests to finance the purchase of residential investment properties. Given the volatility of the stock market in recent years and the very low interest paid on investments such as bank certificates of deposit, a rented residential property is considered by many individuals to be a good investment. Building contractors who are experienced with residential construction and improvements can expand their contracting business with purchases of rental properties. Their skills in the construction field allow them to maintain and improve the rental properties at a low cost. Employees and professionals also supplement their salaries by acquiring rental properties to earn rental income and benefit from the appreciation in property values. Bank lenders will often not allow their small-business lending staff to handle residential-investment-property mortgage loans. Bank management considers the loans to be more suited for handling by their real estate lending staff. The applicant's personal financial condition, personal credit score, and employment income are important factors in the decision by the bank to approve or decline a residential-investment-property mortgage request. Risks and other considerations in this type of business are covered below.

The first risk of residential property ownership is the possibility that the property will decline in value. Refer to page 22 in the *business description* section, which describes the importance of the location of the business. Business and economic conditions in an area have a significant impact upon both residential and business property values. High unemployment in an area can have a negative effect upon residential property values. However, it is very important to understand that banks can be severely criticized and penalized by their bank examiners if there is evidence that the bank is reluctant to lend in low-income areas and discriminates against low-income applicants. Renting a property to a low-income family provides a very important benefit to the community. Investors in properties with low-income renters can be successful if they are not absentee landlords and keep in close touch with the property and its occupant. It is also important that a real estate investor becomes active in the communities where properties are owned. The property value of the rented residence is a primary factor in the bank lender's review of the mortgage loan request. The amount of the loan will usually be not greater than 75% to 80% of the appraised property value.

A second risk in the residential investment property business is the deterioration in the property condition. High maintenance and repair expenses will reduce the cash flow of a property to a point where the investment cannot generate enough cash flow to repay the mortgage loan. See the presentation of the property cash flow in the final part of this section. Property repairs are a labor-intensive activity. The cost to complete the repairs can put the property into a negative cash flow position.

A third risk in the residential investment property business is the possibility that the renter becomes delinquent in their monthly rental payments. A delinquent renter can also be negligent or destructive while living in the property. The process of evicting a delinquent renter can be time-consuming with the need of an attorney to complete the process. A legal expense is another drain on the cash flow of the investor.

RENT-ROLL SCHEDULE

A rent-roll schedule is one of the two most important financial statements that a real estate investor should prepare and submit to the bank. The other statement is a property cash flow, which is also shown in this section. The rent-roll schedule shows the important financial factors that determine the cash flow of each property owned. An example of a rent-roll schedule for an investor owning four residential rental properties follows.

Property	Value	Mortgage Lender	Mortgage Amount	Annual Rent	Annual Mtge. Pay	Real Est. Tax	Maint. Repairs	Insurance & Other Exp.	Net Cash Flow
Phelps	$90,000	Citadel	$42,000	$10,200	$4,300	$1,400	$1,500	$1,000	$2,000
Pierce	$100,000	PNC	$50,000	$10,800	$5,900	$1,600	$1,800	$1,100	$400
Welsh	$80,000	M&T	$25,000	$8,600	$3,600	$1,300	$1,400	$800	$1,500
James	$110,000	M&T	$55,000	$11,160	$5,360	$1,900	$1,600	$1,200	$1,100
Total	$380,000		$172,000	$40,760	$19,160	$6,200	$6,300	$4,100	$5,000

PROPERTY CASH FLOW

Gross rent	$40,760
Real estate tax	($6,200)
Maintenance/repairs	($6,300)
Other expenses	($4,100)
Property cash flow	$24,160
Mortgage debt service	$19,160
Excess cash flow	$5,000
Debt coverage ratio	1.26×

Bankers compute a ratio known as the *loan-to-value ratio*. The ratio compares the level of outstanding mortgage debt to the property values. In the above case, the ratio of 45.2% is considerably lower than the maximum advance permitted by banks of 75% to 80%. Another ratio known as the *debt coverage ratio* compares the property cash flow before the deduction of mortgage payments to the level of mortgage payments. The ratio in the above case of 1.26× is acceptable to bank lenders. The ratio would be much tighter if the properties had a higher level of mortgage indebtedness. It is important that the property owner does not accumulate a high level of mortgage debt to a point that market rents less the property expenses do not provide a satisfactory level of cash flow to repay the debt.

A Good Presentation

The purpose of this guide is to help the small-business owner(s) review their business and evaluate its operating performance, cash flow, financial condition, and borrowing needs. The guide will also provide insight into how the bank lender completes an assessment of the loan request and reaches a decision to approve or decline the loan request. The guide helps the owner(s) prepare the loan application package and anticipate questions that the lender will probably ask. It is important that the applicant is familiar with the analysis that the lender will complete and how the analysis impacts the approval decision.

WRITTEN PORTION OF THE PRESENTATION

The owners do not need to write a "book" as part of the loan presentation. It is not the intention of this guide to create the need for the applicant to do a lot of "busy work." Statement spreadsheets are a recommended part of an application package, although they can be in a summary form that only shows the primary revenues, expenses, assets, and liabilities of the business. The analysis of statement spreads is a normal practice of the lender, and it also helps the applicant identify changes and trends in the business operations and financial condition.

A clear and concise narrative containing three to five pages will help the lender complete their review of the loan request and reduce the turnaround time from the initial request to a final decision. A number of items covered in this guide can probably be explained verbally in order to shorten the length of the written presentation. The following pages are examples of loan request presentations that cover the main points that the lender is looking for. The length of the presentations is not excessive. The presentation should provide the following descriptions and explanations:

1. The legal form of the business and when it was formed
2. The loan(s) requested including the purpose and benefit to the business
3. A description of the products or services and the customer base
4. How the business operates and markets its products (see the business description section)
5. Who the owners are, their experience and accomplishments
6. A financial summary showing operating results and how the business will be able to repay the requested loan(s)

The following schedules should be included in the narrative:

1. Sources and uses of funds statement
2. Debt schedule
3. Collateral schedule
4. Listing of existing legal agreements

ATTACHMENTS

1. Two years' tax returns or CPA-prepared annual statements for the business.
2. An interim year-to-date financial statement prepared by the owner(s) (possibly completed on available software such as QuickBooks).
3. An income statement projection for the next twelve months.
4. A cash flow projection. (This would only be needed if it is necessary to indicate the timing of a specific borrowing need in the next twelve months. The projection can also indicate how the amount borrowed can be repaid.)
5. A balance sheet projection (this would only be needed if the financial condition will change significantly in the next twelve months).
6. An accounts receivable aging.
7. An accounts payable aging.
8. A jobs-in-process schedule (for contractors).
9. Two years' personal tax returns for each owner.
10. A personal financial statement for each owner completed on the bank's form.

Sample Presentations

Rita's Casual Wear LLC

Dakin's Miniatures

Houser Designers, Inc.

Metal Specialists, Inc.

Kelly Equipment Repairs Inc.

Rita's Casual Wear LLC

RITA BOYD, MANAGING MEMBER AND OWNER
DOWNINGTOWN, PA

BUSINESS SUMMARY

Formed April 2005 as an LLC.
Rita Boyd 100% owner.
The business is a retail clothing store at one location in Downingtown, PA.

LOAN REQUESTED

A $50,000 working capital line of credit is requested to support inventory purchases in the fall of the year leading up to the busy holiday season in December. Inventory purchases are also at an increased level in the late summer to meet customer demand at the beginning of the school year. The LLC presently does not have a line of credit from a bank. Rita Boyd has provided financing to support inventory purchases from her own funds. Rita is now making tuition payments for her daughter, and continued personal advances to the business would cause her personal liquidity to be too tight. An income statement and cash flow projection is presented below indicating that borrowings on the line of credit can be fully repaid by the end of 2012. Sales in the final weeks of the year will provide sufficient cash flow to accomplish payment in full. Rita will support the requested line of credit with her personal guaranty. All business assets of the LLC are available to secure the loan. Presently there is no indebtedness due banks or other parties.

BUSINESS DESCRIPTION

The business is a specialty retailer that concentrates on a product line consisting of shirts and sweatshirts that are lettered with the name of a college, high school, or sports team in the local Chester County area. A logo is also included with the lettering. The retail store also sells gently used clothing in good condition on a consignment basis. The clothing is supplied by families in the area. Rita Boyd is selective with this inventory and prefers clothing with known brand names. The customer base is presently broken down into the following categories:

1. Sales of lettered clothing to retail customers, payable in cash: 60% of 2012 sales.
2. Sales of lettered clothing to school districts, colleges, and sports teams in the area. Thirty-day credit terms are available: 20% of 2012 sales.
3. Sales of used consignment clothing: 20% of 2012 sales.

The business has been able to increase sales modestly in a period when household and organization budgets have been tight. Sales of lettered clothing to schools, colleges, and teams have been the primary reason for the modest sales growth. The retail business has gained a good reputation as a supplier of sports-related clothing. Clothing wholesalers with the capability to letter/embroider their stock have been the suppliers to the business. The primary supplier is located in nearby Coatesville. Two other suppliers are also available in the Philadelphia area. The cost of inventory has been stable in the last three years. Thirty-day credit terms are available.

The store is located within the Borough of Downingtown on a heavily traveled two-lane road. The business has occupied the store property since its formation in 2005. The present lease expires in 2015. Customer parking is available in a nearby municipal lot. The Downingtown area is a growing community with several nearby business parks and shopping centers. The recession slowed the residential building in the area, although that activity is now picking up. Rita Boyd has been the sole owner of the business. She is assisted by three part-time employees at the store, who also handle phone orders and orders on the website. Rita is active in the sales effort at the store and calls upon the local school districts and colleges to solicit their clothing orders for the fall, winter, and spring seasons. Rita keeps up-to-date with a mailing list of past customers and occasionally mails out flyers and coupons.

FINANCIAL SUMMARY

	Income Statement				*Balance Sheet*	
	Actual 2010	Actual 2011	Actual 1/1-6/30/12	Projected 7/1-12/31/12	Actual 12/31/11	
Revenues	$233,000	$240,384	$90,000	$219,000	Cash	$20,000
Gross profit	$116,500	$125,000	$40,500	$98,500	Accounts receiv.	$5,000
GP margin	50%	52%	45%	45%	Inventory	$16,000
Owner's salary	$45,000	$48,000	$24,000	$24,000	Total current assets	$41,000
Other salaries	$22,000	$27,000	$10,000	$20,000	Fixed assets	$20,000
Rent expense	$24,000	$24,000	$12,000	$12,000	Total assets	$61,000
Other expenses	$9,000	$11,000	$6,000	$6,000	Notes payable	$0
Operating profit	$16,500	$15,000	($11,500)	$36,500	Accounts payable	$10,000
					Other current liab.	$2,000
					Total current liab.	$12,000
					Net worth	$49,000
					Total liabs. + net worth	$61,000

Cash Flow Projection from 7/1/2012 to 12/31/2012

	July	Aug.	Sept.	Oct.	Nov.	Dec.
Cash sales	$15,000	$25,000	$20,000	$20,000	$40,000	$50,000
Accts. receiv. collected	$0	$0	$20,000	$16,000	$3,000	$5,000
Total cash received	$15,000	$25,000	$40,000	$36,000	$43,000	$55,000
Payments for inventory	$8,300	$57,200	$0	$0	$55,000	$6,000
Owner's salary	$4,000	$4,000	$4,000	$4,000	$4,000	$4,000
Other salaries	$0	$4,000	$4,000	$4,000	$4,000	$4,000
Other operating expenses	$3,000	$3,000	$3,000	$3,000	$3,000	$3,000
Total cash paid	$15,300	$68,200	$11,000	$11,000	$66,000	$17,000
Surplus/deficit	($300)	($43,200)	$29,000	$25,000	($23,000)	$38,000
Cumulative	($300)	($43,500)	($14,500)	$10,500	($12,500)	$25,500
Line of credit		$50,000 borrowed in Aug.			Repaid in full in Dec	

Financial Analysis

The business had no borrowings outstanding as of December 31, 2011. Line of credit borrowings will total $50,000 at the end of August to pay supplier invoices for inventory purchased for projected sales at the beginning of the school year. Inventory purchases will also be high in November to meet holiday sales. Cash flow from seasonal sales in the holiday season will be sufficient to repay line of credit borrowings in full by the end of 2012.

The retail business will continue to be profitable with sales growth of 28% projected in 2012. The second half of the year is the most profitable due to seasonal demand at the beginning of the school year and during the holidays. Increased sales to high schools and colleges plus a higher level of consumer spending are expected in 2012. The gross profit margin will decline slightly with the cause being increases in lower margin sales to high schools and colleges. The level of owner's compensation totaling $48,000 is adequate to meet personal living expenses and personal loan payments.

AVAILABLE BUSINESS ASSET COLLATERAL

Accounts receivable and inventory of the retail business are available to secure the requested $50,000 line of credit. The business is seasonal with the largest inventory purchases occurring in the late summer to support sales at the beginning of the school year and during the holiday season. Accounts receivable billings to high schools, colleges, and local teams will occur in August for inventory purchased for the fall and winter seasons, and in February for spring sports teams. A summary of accounts receivable and inventory collateral is as follows:

Category	*Amt. on 12/31/11* *Balance Sheet*	*Comment*
Accounts receivable	$5,000	Peak of approx. $40,000 in Sept. & Oct.
Inventory	$16,000	Peak of approx. $70,000 in Sept. and Nov.

PERSONAL FINANCIAL CONDITION OF RITA BOYD

See the attached personal financial statement on the bank's form. Highlights of the personal financial condition are as follows:

Personal liquid assets: $20,000 in a money market account
$15,000 in a bond mutual fund

Personal residence: $180,000 approximate value subject to a $90,000 mortgage

Personal debts: $90,000 mortgage due PNC Bank. Monthly payment of $540
$12,000 auto loan due Ford Credit. Monthly payment of $260
$2,000 in credit cards to be paid off within 60 days

ATTACHMENTS

1. 2010 and 2011 tax returns for Rita's Casual Wear LLC
2. Income statement projection for 2012
3. Cash flow projection for 2012
4. 2010 and 2011 tax returns for Rita Boyd
5. Personal financial statement on the bank's form

Dakin's Miniatures

Roberta Dakin, Proprietor
Searsport, Maine

Business Summary

Business is a proprietorship that started operations in 2002.

Roberta Dakin is the sole proprietor.

The business builds wooden crafts for sales to retail gift stores.

Current plans are to open a retail gift store at their current business location that is not in the same market area as their current retail gift-store customers.

Loan Requested

A $50,000 term loan is requested to renovate a portion of the current business property into a retail store. The initial six months period of the loan term should allow for periodic borrowings up to a total of $50,000 to finance the cost of the project. This initial borrowing period should only require monthly payments of interest. At the end of the initial six-month period, monthly principal and interest payments can be made on a five-year amortization. The new store will sell wooden crafts that are built by the business consisting of ship and boat models, lighthouse models, and other harbor scenes. A sources and uses of funds statement follows:

Sources of Funds		Uses of Funds		
Bank loan	$50,000	Renovations	$30,000	
Owner's cash	$20,000	Tools	$5,000	
Total	$70,000	Materials	$20,000	(wood)
		Salary (new employee)	$15,000	(six months until new store opens)
		Total	$70,000	

The loan will allow the business to increase and diversify its sales. Presently sales are significantly concentrated with one gift store, consisting of 60% of annual sales and two others making up the balance of annual sales. The current customers are located in a distant area and will not compete with the new store. The loan will be personally guaranteed by Roberta Dakin and her husband Emery. Available security will be all business assets (with the exception of a truck that secures an existing loan) and a first mortgage covering the business property being renovated (owned by Roberta and Emery Dakin).

BUSINESS DESCRIPTION

The wooden crafts business currently sells to a gift store located in York, Maine. This store has been the largest customer and is located in a beach resort area in Southern Maine. Roberta Dakin was introduced to the store owner by her sister who lives in the area. Another store in Southern Maine and a store located in New Hampshire make up the balance of the existing customer base. The retail gift stores are seasonal businesses with sales concentrated in the summer months. Summer vacationers are the primary customers. The new Searsport retail store will have a similar target market. Summer visitors continue to be attracted to the area, and many drive through town as they travel farther up the coast. No other gift stores in the area will carry the crafts that the business builds. The wooden models are a unique inventory item. Roberta Dakin and one existing full-time employee build the models at a business property in Searsport, Maine, which used to be occupied by a residential builder that went out of business. Roberta delivers the models to her customers by truck and meets frequently with the gift-store owners to determine their purchasing plans. With the addition of the new retail store in Searsport, Roberta plans to hire an additional full-time employee with experience building crafts. The new employee will also work in the retail store. Roberta's husband (Emery) is employed at a local chemical plant in a production position. He assists at the crafts business during the weekend.

FINANCIAL SUMMARY

Income Statement

The budget for the new retail store is for the first twelve months after the store is opened. The twelve months projection for the entire business covers the same period. The new employee will earn an annual salary of $30,000. Rita Dakin's annual distribution will remain $25,000.

	Actual 2011	Actual 2012	Budget (New Store)	12-Month Projection
Sales	$119,000	$147,000	$73,000	$220,000
Material costs	$41,700	$44,000	$23,000	$67,000
Gross profit	$77,300 (65%)	$103,000 (70%)	$50,000 (68%)	$153,000 (70%)
Employee salaries	$30,000	$35,000		$65,000
Vehicle expense	$15,000	$19,000		$22,000
Utilities/phone	$6,800	$8,000		$9,000
Interest expense	$500	$1,000		$3,500
Other expenses	$5,000	$6,000		$7,000
Net profit	$20,000	$34,000		$46,500
NP + interest exp.	$20,500	$35,000		$50,000
Distributions to R. Dakin	($20,000)	($25,000)		($25,000)
NP + interest exp. minus distributions (Business cash flow)	$500	$10,000		$25,000

Debt Schedule

Lender	Original Amount	Present Balance	Monthly Payment	Security
Bangor Savings	$18,000	$15,000	$358	Truck
Requested term loan	$50,000	$50,000 when settled	approx $975	Mortgage & all business assets

Total annual debt service: $16,000 approx.

Debt Service Coverage

	Actual 2012	12-month projection
Net profit + interest expense	$35,000	$50,000
Less: Distributions to R. Dakin	($25,000)	($25,000)
Business cash flow	$10,000	$25,000
Projected debt service	$16,000	$16,000
Excess (deficit) cash flow	($6,000)	$9,000

Balance Sheet

The $50,000 loan and the $20,000 equity contribution of the owner provide funding for the renovations and the increased inventory of wood. The loan and equity contribution also are used to increase the cash balance to pay the new employee and purchase tools.

	As of 12/31/12	Projected	(as of the date the $50,000 loan is fully drawn)
Cash	$20,000	$25,000	
Accounts receiv.	$15,000	$15,000	
Inventory	$5,000	$40,000	
Total current assets	$40,000	$80,000	
Tools & equip.	$5,000	$10,000	
Vehicles	$17,000	$17,000	
Improvements to business property	$0	$30,000	(The real estate is owned by R. & E. Dakin. The new improvements are considered a business asset.)
Total assets	$62,000	$137,000	
Accounts payable	$1,000	$6,000	
Other current liabs.	$2,000	$2,000	
Total current liabs.	$3,000	$8,000	
Vehicle loan	$15,000	$14,000	
Bank term loan	$0	$50,000	
Total liabilities	$18,000	$72,000	
Net worth	$44,000	$65,000	
Total liabs. + NW	$62,000	$137,000	

Financial Analysis

The new retail store is projected to increase the revenues of the wooden crafts business by 50%. Roberta Dakin feels that her projection for the new store is realistic. She has been able to talk with other gift-store owners in the area and feels that the lack of competition for the special type of wooden crafts that the business builds justifies the $73,000 first-year annual sales projection. The new employee will increase the level of production in the business. Projected business cash flow (net profit + interest expense less distributions to Roberta Dakin) is adequate to cover annual payments on the debt of the business shown in the debt schedule.

AVAILABLE COLLATERAL FOR THE $50,000 LOAN

Asset	Approximate Value
Business real estate	Acquisition cost of $50,000 in 2005
First lien mortgage	Approximate value of $100,000 after completion of improvements
Tools and equipment	$10,000 see projected balance sheet

Roberta and Emery Dakin purchased the business property at a sheriff's sale. The building was empty. It was previously occupied by a builder that went out of business. They improved the property with personal funds after the purchase. After completion of the $30,000 in improvements for the new retail store, the estimated value will be $100,000. This value adequately covers the requested $50,000 loan.

PERSONAL FINANCIAL CONDITION OF ROBERTA AND EMERY DAKIN

Personal Income
$25,000 distributions from wooden crafts business
$40,000 salary from chemical plant
$65,000 total

Liquid Assets
$40,000 in cash at Bangor Savings Bank

Real Estate Owned
Residence with a value of $160,000 subject to an existing mortgage of $120,000
Wooden crafts business property with a value of $100,000 after completion of the planned improvements

Personal debt
$120,000 residential mortgage with a monthly payment of $740
$10,000 auto loan with a monthly payment of $240

ATTACHMENTS

1. 2011 and 2012 personal tax returns including schedule C for the wooden crafts business
2. Personal financial statement on the bank's form
3. Income statement and balance sheet projection
4. Photographs of the business property

Houser Designers, Inc.

DAVID HOUSER, PRESIDENT AND OWNER
WAYNE, PA

BUSINESS SUMMARY

S corporation formed in 1994.

100% owned by David Houser.

The business provides interior design and remodeling services. Services include project design and installation of the planned improvements.

The customer base consists of home owners and small office buildings.

LOANS REQUESTED

A $300,000 commercial mortgage is requested to purchase the office building that the business has occupied since 2003. A $375,000 purchase price has been finalized with the present owner. The existing lease will expire in six months, and there is a strong possibility that the current monthly rental payment of $2,000 will be increased. A mortgage amortization of twenty years is requested. The monthly principal and interest payment would be similar to the monthly rent currently being paid.

Houser Designers would like to continue with the $100,000 working capital line of credit currently offered by the bank. The business has recently been the winning bidder on a business office remodeling project of a local bank. The bank desires to redesign and remodel the second floor of the building that will consist of six offices, a conference room, a central area, and a small room for files. The bank operates a branch banking office on the first floor. The contract totals $300,000 for design and installation of the improvements. A cash flow is included in this presentation that indicates that an additional $100,000 working capital loan is needed for the job that will take four months to complete. Subcontractors and material suppliers will need to be paid before the majority of contract billings are paid by the bank. The additional $100,000 working capital loan is required because the present $100,000 line of credit will not provide enough borrowing availability to cover the costs of the project. The cash flow projection indicates that the gross profit of the bank project will be a significant $75,000. The project will be a major contributor to the total gross profit earned in 2013.

BUSINESS DESCRIPTION

The interior design and remodeling business initially designs the project. The business works closely with the property owner to have the improvements meet the owner's needs at a cost that the owner can afford. The job will then proceed with the construction and installation of the planned improvements. The property owner benefits from having the project design and installation completed by one provider. In the current marketplace, the design and installation of a remodeling project often involves two separate companies. David Houser enjoys good relationships with lumber and drywall suppliers in the area. He also has worked closely with remodeling contractors, painters, and electricians, who are the subcontractors that complete the improvements. The good working relationships enable the business to obtain low prices from the suppliers and subcontractors. The total project cost can be finalized into an affordable range.

The customer base has shifted in the last two years to a larger portion of revenues being commercial work. The project mix (as a percent of revenues) is as follows:

	2011	2012
Residential	60%	45%
Office buildings	40%	55%

The office building jobs usually involve a competitive bid. Preparation of the bid has taken up a greater portion of David Houser's time. He also gives priority to marketing and management. David enjoys a strong reputation as an interior designer in the local area. The business also employs a full-time interior designer, who also has a good reputation. The other key employee is a project manager who coordinates with the suppliers and subcontractors, and reviews and manages the job costs.

FINANCIAL SUMMARY

Income Statement

	2011 Actual	2012 Actual
Revenues	$1,050,000	$1,146,000
Gross profit	$302,000 (29%)	$332,000 (29%)
Owner's salary	$60,000	$60,000
Other salaries	$122,000	$128,000
Other expenses	$74,000	$86,000
Rent	$24,000	$24,000
Interest expense	$7,000	$5,000
Depreciation exp.	$10,000	$10,000
Net profit	$5,000	$19,000
NP + interest + depreciation + rent (business cash flow)	$46,000	$58,000

Note: Rent is added back in this calculation as the business property will be purchased, and rent will no longer be payable.

Cash Flow Projection for Bank Remodeling Contract

	March 2013	April 2013	May 2013	June 2013	Total
Collections of billings	$0	$75,000	$100,000	$125,000	$300,000
Payments (subcontractors)	($30,000)	($30,000)	($30,000)	($30,000)	($120,000)
Payments (materials)	($60,000)	($45,000)	$0	$0	($105,000)
Surplus (deficit)	($90,000)	$0	$70,000	$95,000	$75,000
Requested loan	$100,000 borrowed in March. Loan will be repaid in June.				

Debt Schedule

Type Loan	Amount	Present Balance	Annual Payment	Security
Existing line of credit	$100,000	$70,000	$3,800 interest (estimate)	Business assets
Requested loan for bank contract	$100,000	$100,000 when settled	$1,200 interest (estimate: 4 months)	Business assets
Mortgage request	$300,000	$300,000 when settled	$26,000	Business property

(Borrower on the mortgage will be David Houser who will own the real estate)

$31,000 total estimated debt service

Debt Service Coverage

Business cash flow is measured by the total of net profit + depreciation + interest + rent expense. Rent expense is added back due to the fact that rent will no longer be payable. The analysis below compares business cash flow (as calculated for 2011 and 2012) to estimated interest expense on the working capital loans, the annual mortgage payments, plus real estate taxes and property insurance that the business will now have to pay. Operating results for both 2011 and 2012 indicate a satisfactory ability to repay the proposed debt.

	2011	2012
Business cash flow	$46,000	$58,000
Estimated interest exp.		($5,000)
Annual mortgage payments		($26,000)
Annual real estate taxes		($3,000)
Annual insurance		($1,000)
Total payments		($35,000)
Excess cash flow		$23,000

Balance Sheet

	12/31/11	12/31/12	
Cash	$50,000	$79,000	
Accounts receivable	$130,000	$140,000	
Revenues not billed	$45,000	$50,000	(booked revenues under percentage of completion accounting, but not yet billed)
Inventory	$10,000	$10,000	
Total current assets	$235,000	$279,000	
Vehicles & equipment	$40,000	$30,000	
Total assets	$275,000	$309,000	
Accounts payable	$60,000	$60,000	
Line of credit borrowed	$65,000	$70,000	
Other current liabs.	$10,000	$20,000	
Total current liabs.	$135,000	$150,000	
Long-term debt	$0	$0	
Total liabilities	$135,000	$150,000	
Net worth	$140,000	$159,000	
Total liabs. + NW	$275,000	$309,000	
Working capital	$100,000	$129,000	
Current ratio	1.74×	1.86×	
Total liabs. / net worth	0.96×	0.94×	

Accounts Receivable Aging (for 12/31/12)

Name	Balance owed	1-30	Days from the invoice date 31-60	61-90	over 90
Davis Offices	$50,000	$35,000	$15,000		
Price Offices	$27,000	$18,000	$9,000		
Various residents	$63,000	$48,000	$15,000		
Total	$140,000	$101,000	$39,000		

Financial Analysis

As noted above under "Debt Service Coverage," business cash flow in 2011 and 2012 is at a sufficient level to cover the loan payments required on the proposed loans. The increase in revenues in the office remodeling portion of the business caused a slight increase in revenues in 2012. While bidding is competitive, accurate cost estimates and good cost management allowed the gross profit margin to be stable. The $300,000 bank remodeling job will provide a good contribution to 2013 gross profits. The requested $100,000 working capital loan will be paid in full from the cash flow of the contract. The financial condition of the business is good with a current ratio of 1.86×. All accounts payable to subcontractors and material suppliers have been paid within thirty days of the invoice date. The business has no long-term debt.

AVAILABLE COLLATERAL

Commercial Mortgage ($300,000)

Property	Value
Office building to be purchased (to be owned by David Houser) Lincoln Highway Wayne, PA	$375,000 (purchase price)

$100,000 line of credit and $100,000 working capital loan

Asset	Value
Accounts receivable	$140,000 (balance sheet for 12/31/12) $300,000 (to be billed on bank project)

PERSONAL FINANCIAL CONDITION OF DAVID HOUSER

Personal income	*Personal liquid assets*
$60,000 salary from Houser Designers, Inc.	$40,000 in money market account $40,000 in mutual funds

Real estate owned	*Personal indebtedness*
Residence valued at $240,000	$150,000 residential mortgage (monthly payment of $1,400) $40,000 home equity line of credit (present balance of $10,000)

ATTACHMENTS

1. 2011 and 2012 tax returns for Houser Designers, Inc.
2. Cash flow projection for bank contract
3. Accounts receivable aging
4. 2011 and 2012 personal tax returns for David Houser
5. Copy of agreement of sale for the business property
6. Personal financial statement for David Houser on the bank's form

Metal Specialists, Inc.

CRAIG TAYLOR, PRESIDENT AND 50% OWNER
ROBERT ELLIS, VICE PRESIDENT AND 50% OWNER
POTTSTOWN, PA

BUSINESS SUMMARY

S corporation formed in 2006.
50% owned by Craig Taylor.
50% owned by Robert Ellis.
The business fabricates metal parts and attachments.
The customer base consists of trucking companies, utilities, food
processors, and farms.

LOANS REQUESTED

Metal Specialists requests a $50,000 five-year term loan to
purchase the following equipment:

Lathe and turret punch press	cost $45,000
Milling machine	cost $18,000
	Total cost $63,000

The equipment will increase the productivity of the fabrication
business and reduce the time that it takes to complete purchase orders.
The business has experienced an increase in orders from the existing
customer base, and its order backlog has increased to $480,000
compared to $300,000 at this time last year.

The increased backlog has caused Metal Specialists to also request an increase in their working capital line from $200,000 to $300,000.

BUSINESS DESCRIPTION

Metal Specialists fabricates metal parts and accessories that are used primarily as attachments to trucks, agricultural equipment, and food processing equipment. No one customer has consisted of more than 20% of annual sales. The customer base provides a steady stream of repeat orders, although the size of the order will vary depending upon the capital budget of the customer. East Penn Utilities, Smith Trucking, Turner Tree Removal, and numerous Lancaster and Berks County farms have been the leading customers over the last three years.

The business operates from a plant leased from Schaffer Sheet Metal Co. The plant is part of a large business property that includes Schaffer Sheet Metal, Metal Specialists, and an excavating contractor. The present lease requires monthly payments of $3,000 with an expiration date of 2016. The metal fabrication business is equipment intensive. Metal Specialists has acquired with bank and lease financing the following equipment:

1. Lathe
2. Milling machine
3. Tube and pipe bender
4. Metal-forming and cutting machines

The two owners meet regularly to review the business plans and agendas for the week. Craig Taylor devotes the majority of his time to marketing and customer communications. He also manages the recording of financial data into computer software and monitors the financial trends on a regular basis. He works with the firm's CPA (Tom Beasler), who prepares an annual compilation financial statement. The CPA also reviews the recorded financial information and actively discusses trends and issues with Craig and Robert Ellis. Robert Ellis devotes most of his time to operations and production. He also does the purchasing from three available steel suppliers. He watches their prices closely for changes and trends. Steel prices have increased 3% per annum over the last two years.

FINANCIAL SUMMARY

Income Statement

	2011	2012	Projection 2013
Revenues	$1,217,142	$1,226,316	$1,336,684
Gross profit	$426,000 (35%)	$466,000 (38%)	$507,940 (38%)
Owners' salaries	$140,000	$150,000	$150,000
Admin salaries	$60,000	$65,000	$70,000
Rent expense	$36,000	$36,000	$36,000
Other expenses	$110,000	$120,000	$130,000
Interest expense	$25,000	$19,000	$25,000
Depreciation expense	$65,000	$60,000	$65,000
Net profit	($10,000)	$16,000	$31,940
NP + depreciation + interest exp. (Business cash flow)	$80,000	$95,000	$121,940

Debt Schedule

Loan	Original Amount	Present Balance	Annual Payments	Security
Requested term loan	$50,000	$50,000 when settled	$11,700	Lathe Milling machine
Requested line of credit	$300,000 requested	$200,000	$9,000 estimated interest	Accounts receiv. inventory
Existing term loan	$60,000	$40,000	$14,000	Cutting machines
Various capital leases	various	$115,000	$37,300	Leased equipment
Total		$405,000	$72,000	

Debt Service Coverage

	Actual 2012	Projected 2013
Business cash flow (net profit + deprec. + interest)	$95,000	$121,940
Annual debt service	$72,000	$72,000
Debt coverage ratio	1.31×	1.69×

Balance Sheet

	12/31/11	12/31/12
Cash	$20,000	$36,000
Accounts receivable	$180,000	$250,000
Inventory	$66,000	$106,000
Total current assets	$266,000	$392,000
Equipment	$300,000	$240,000
Total assets	$566,000	$632,000
Accounts payable	$80,000	$80,000
Line of credit borrowed	$120,000	$200,000
Other current liabilities	$15,000	$15,000
Total current liabilities	$215,000	$295,000
Capital leases	$135,000	$115,000
Term loan	$50,000	$40,000
Total liabilities	$400,000	$450,000
Net worth	$166,000	$182,000
Total liabs. + NW	$566,000	$632,000
Working capital	$51,000	$97,000
Current ratio	1.24×	1.33×
Total liabs. / NW	2.41×	2.47×

Accounts Receivable Aging
for 12/31/2012

Account	1-30 days	31-60 days	61-90 days	over 90 days	Total
		Days outstanding from invoice date			
Turner Tree	$0	$20,000	$20,000	$5,000	$45,000
Various farms	$10,000	$10,000	$10,000	$5,000	$35,000
County Trucking	$20,000	$10,000	$10,000	$0	$40,000
All others	$80,000	$35,000	$15,000	$0	$130,000
Total	$110,000	$75,000	$55,000	$10,000	$250,000

Accounts Payable Aging
for 12/31/2012

Supplier	1-30 days	31-60 days	Total
	Days outstanding from invoice date		
Tyson Steel	$40,000	$10,000	$50,000
Rail Steel	$14,000	$6,000	$20,000
Others	$10,000		$10,000
Total	$64,000	$16,000	$80,000

Financial Analysis

Revenues in 2012 were flat compared to 2011. However, orders from existing customers increased significantly in the second half of 2012, and shipments in the last quarter of 2012 were higher than any previous quarter since 2008. Conversations with customers have indicated that the customer base is planning increased capital expenditures for the first time since the recession began in 2008. Steel prices trended slightly higher in 2012. Good pricing and increased productivity (lower labor costs per unit) caused the gross profit margin to improve from 35% to 38%. The strong backlog as of December 31, 2012, should lead to higher revenues and profits in 2013. Stable gross profit margins are expected given the improvement in productivity and the effective use of equipment. Business cash flow will be sufficient to meet payments on the term loans and capital leases.

The accounts receivable aging as of December 31, 2012, showed some slowness. A tree-removal business and several farmers are usually slow pay in the winter months. Management will meet with the slow-paying customers to attempt to speed up their payments. Faster collections would reduce the usage on the line of credit. The working capital position as of December 31, 2012, is somewhat tight with a current ratio of 1.33×. The working capital position should improve with the increase in business cash flow projected in 2013.

AVAILABLE COLLATERAL

Line of Credit ($300,000)		*Term Loan ($50,000)*	
Accounts receivable	$250,000 at 12/31/12	Lathe / turret punch press	$45,000 purchase price
Inventory	$106,000 at 12/31/12	Milling machine	$18,000 purchase price
	$356,000 total		$63,000 total

PERSONAL FINANCIAL CONDITION

	Craig Taylor	*Robert Ellis*
Personal income	$75,000 (Metal Specialists)	$75,000 (Metal Specialists)
Liquid assets	$90,000 (cash & mutual funds)	$50,000 (cash)
Real estate owned	$325,000 residence	$350,000 residence
Personal debt	$210,000 mortgage ($1,410 per month) $20,000 auto loan ($380 per month)	$250,000 mortgage ($1,500 per month) $20,000 home equity line ($10,000 balance)

ATTACHMENTS

1. 12/31/11 and 12/31/12 CPA compilation statements for Metal Specialists, Inc.
2. 2013 projection for Metal Specialists, Inc.
3. Accounts receivable and accounts payable agings for Metal Specialists, Inc.
4. 2011 and 2012 tax returns for Craig Taylor and Robert Ellis
5. Personal financial statements for Craig Taylor and Robert Ellis (on bank's form)

Kelly Equipment Repairs Inc.

Brian Kelly, president and 100% owner
Morgantown, PA

Business Summary

S corporation formed in 2005.

100% owned by Brian Kelly.

The business services and repairs mowers, tractors, and other gasoline-powered equipment used by home owners, landscapers, small contractors, and farmers.

The business sells repair parts and tools used by the same customer base.

Loans Requested

Kelly Equipment Repairs requests a $100,000 term loan to finance the purchase of an equipment-repair business located in nearby New Holland, PA, that services the farming community in the Lancaster County area. A $50,000 line of credit is also requested to meet the working capital needs of the expanded business. The business acquired will become a part of Kelly Equipment Repairs Inc. The purchased business will retain its existing trade name and will be known as Kelly Equipment Repairs Inc. d.b.a. Moyer Farm Equipment. The business purchase will enable Kelly Equipment Repairs to penetrate the local farm-equipment repairs market. Kelly is currently generating only a modest amount of sales in this market. The business purchase will include the inventory, equipment, customer list, and business name of the existing Moyer Farm Equipment business. Accounts receivable of Moyer Farm Equipment will not be included in the sale. A line of credit in the amount of $50,000 is needed to support the anticipated increased inventory and accounts receivable levels of the combined businesses. Kelly Equipment Repairs has expanded its revenues to landscapers and small contractors. Kelly offers thirty-day credit terms but has noticed that some customers take as long as sixty days to pay the balance due. Moyer Farm Equipment has also offered thirty-day credit terms to farmers and has also experienced payments that have extended beyond the thirty-day period. Residential customers of Kelly Equipment Repairs continue to pay cash or use their credit card for equipment servicing and repairs. A sources and uses of funds statement follows:

Sources	Uses
$50,000 line of credit	$50,000 working capital for expanded business
$100,000 term loan	$20,000 inventory—Moyer Farm Equipment
$20,000 equity contribution	$75,000 equipment—Moyer Farm Equipment
	$25,000 Moyer business name and customer list
$170,000 total sources	$170,000 total uses

BUSINESS DESCRIPTION

The primary source of sales for Kelly Equipment is the servicing and repair of mowers, tractors, and gasoline engines. Equipment servicing and repairs totaled 80% of sales in 2012. The sale of repair parts and small tools made up the remaining 20% of sales. The customer base of Kelly Equipment can be broken down as follows for 2011 and 2012:

	2011	2012
Residence owners	60%	50%
Landscapers	25%	30%
Small contractors	10%	15%
Farmers	5%	5%

Sales to business owners have been the primary reason for the growth in sales in 2012. The Moyer Farm Equipment business purchase will considerably increase the percentage share of sales provided by business customers as Moyer's farm customer base can be classified in the business category. James Moyer has agreed to continue as vice president with management responsibility for Moyer Farm Equipment. He will no longer be a shareholder but will draw the same salary as he did in 2012. James has developed strong working relationships with his farm customer base and is considered a very key employee going forward, as Brian Kelly has given high priority to retaining the customer base at Moyer Farm Equipment.

Kelly Equipment and Moyer Farm Equipment will continue to occupy their respective rented business locations. They have both been long-term tenants at each location. Their locations are very convenient to their customer base. Morgantown and New Holland are not far apart making it easy for employees to work at both locations and be able to respond to changes in the workload.

Brian Kelly has decided to engage Greg Davis, CPA, as the accountant for his expanded business. He has used a different accounting firm for the preparation of annual tax returns but has decided to make a change due to the retirement of the CPA assigned to his account. Brian will ask the new accountant for assistance with the software to be utilized to record all financial transactions. He also will need assistance consolidating the financial records and statements of Moyer Farm Equipment. He would like to improve the monthly reporting of inventory and operating expenses. Brian would also like to have better confidence in the monthly financial statements that he is reviewing and will ask Greg Davis to prepare an annual CPA compilation statement for the corporation.

See the financial summary on the next page.

FINANCIAL SUMMARY

Income Statement

	Kelly Equipment Repairs		Moyer Farm Equipment		Combined After Purchase
	2011	2012	2011	2012	2012
Sales	$755,000	$790,000	$542,000	$571,000	$1,361,000
Gross profit	$362,000	$366,000	$217,000	$240,000	$606,000
Gross profit margin	48%	46%	40%	42%	44%
Officer's salary	$55,000	$62,000	$45,000	$48,000	$110,000
Other salaries	$160,000	$180,000	$100,000	$109,000	$289,000
Rent	$22,000	$24,000	$18,000	$18,000	$42,000
Other operating exp.	$88,000	$60,000	$28,000	$33,000	$93,000
Interest exp.	$0	$0	$0	$0	$6,000
Depreciation	$19,000	$20,000	$15,000	$15,000	$35,000
Net profit	$18,000	$20,000	$11,000	$17,000	$31,000
NP + interest + depreciation (business cash flow)	$37,000	$40,000	$26,000	$32,000	$72,000

Debt Schedule

Loan	Amount	Annual Payment	Security
Requested term loan	$100,000	approx. $23,160	All business assets
Requested line of credit	$50,000	approx. $1,000 (interest only)	All business assets
Total	$150,000	$24,160	

Debt Service Coverage (from 2012 combined income statement)

Net profit + depreciation + interest (business cash flow)	$72,000
Estimated interest on line of credit	($1,000)
Principal and interest on term loan	($23,160)
Total debt service	($24,160)
Excess cash flow	$47,840
Debt service coverage ratio	2.98×

Balance Sheet

	Kelly Equipment 12/31/12	Combined Kelly Equipment & Moyer Farm Equipment (After Purchase)	
Cash	$50,000	$50,000	
Accounts receivable	$50,000	$50,000	
Inventory	$40,000	$60,000	
Total current assets	$140,000	$160,000	
Equipment	$80,000	$155,000	
Business name and customer list	$0	$25,000	
Total assets	$220,000	$340,000	
Accounts payable	$30,000	$30,000	
Notes payable —current portion	$0	$20,000	(first year of principal due on $100,000 term loan)
Other current liabs.	$10,000	$10,000	
Total current liabs.	$40,000	$60,000	
Notes payable —long term	$0	$80,000	(term loan)
Total liabilities	$40,000	$140,000	
Net worth	$180,000	$200,000	($20,000 equity contribution)
Total liabilities + net worth	$220,000	$340,000	
Working capital	$100,000	$100,000	
Current ratio	3.50×	2.67×	
Total liabs. / NW	.22×	.70×	

NOTE: At the time of purchase, there will be a zero balance on the line of credit due to the strong cash balance. The line of credit will be available to support discounted inventory purchases and slower accounts receivable collections.

Accounts Receivable Aging (Kelly Equipment as of 12/31/12)

Account	Days Outstanding from Invoice Date			
	1-30	31-60	61-90	Total
Various landscapers	$25,000	$7,500	$4,500	$37,000
Various contractors	$8,000	$2,000		$10,000
Various farmers	$2,000	$500	$500	$3,000
Total	$35,000	$10,000	$5,000	$50,000

Financial Analysis

Kelly Equipment Repairs Inc. is in a strong financial position to acquire Moyer Farm Equipment. Kelly's December 31, 2012, current ratio is 3.5×, and there are no outstanding borrowed funds. The combined balance sheets after the purchase show a continued strong current ratio of 2.67×. Total liabilities will remain below the level of net worth after the purchase of Moyer, which will be funded by the $100,000 term loan and an equity contribution of $20,000. Both Kelly Equipment and Moyer Farm Equipment have been profitable with a modest amount of sales growth. The equipment repair businesses have had stable gross profit margins. Combined business cash flow of the two businesses provides a strong debt service coverage ratio of 2.98×.

AVAILABLE COLLATERAL FOR $100,000 TERM LOAN AND $50,000 LINE OF CREDIT

Asset	*Value*
Accounts receivable	$50,000 (combined after the purchase)
Inventory	$60,000 (combined after the purchase)
Equipment	$155,000 (combined after the purchase)
Total	$265,000

PERSONAL FINANCIAL CONDITION OF BRIAN KELLY

Income	$62,000 from Kelly Equipment Repairs Inc.
Liquid assets	$60,000 cash
Real estate owned	$230,000 approximate value of residence
Personal debt	$160,000 residential mortgage (monthly payment of $950)
	$15,000 auto loan (monthly payment of $360)

ATTACHMENTS

1. 2011 and 2012 tax returns for Kelly Equipment Repairs Inc.
2. 2011 and 2012 tax returns for Moyer Farm Equipment
3. Combined income statement and balance sheet after the purchase
4. Accounts receivable aging for Kelly Equipment Repairs Inc.
5. 2011 and 2012 personal tax returns for Brian Kelly
6. Personal financial statement for Brian Kelly on the bank's form